Beginner's Guide To Selling Crafts On Etsy 2024.

Step-by-Step Manual for Newcomers to Thrive in the Etsy Marketplace.

Wilson Skylar

Table Of Contents

INTRODUCTION

Welcome to a realm where words weave enchanting tales and stories unfurl like petals in a timeless garden. In this literary sanctuary, every page invites you to embark on a journey that transcends the ordinary and explores the extraordinary. From the first sentence, let the prose be a guide, leading you through landscapes of imagination and characters that will become your companions.

Within these covers, emotions are penned, and adventures unfold, offering solace, excitement, and a kaleidoscope of emotions. Whether you seek an escape from reality or a mirror to reflect upon it, this book endeavors to be both a sanctuary and a mirror, reflecting the myriad facets of the human experience.

So, open your heart to the written symphony, where each chapter is a note, and the narrative orchestrates a melody that resonates with the rhythm of life. Embrace the magic held within these pages, for within this book, stories are not just written; they come alive, beckoning you to immerse yourself in the boundless world of literature.

Welcome to the vibrant and creative world of craft selling on Etsy – an entrepreneurial journey that combines passion with commerce, craftsmanship with community, and artistry with opportunity. In the realm of Etsy, artisans, makers, and creators converge to showcase their unique talents and share their handmade treasures with a global audience.

In this comprehensive guide, we embark on a journey through the intricacies of crafting a successful business on Etsy. From the inception of your creative idea to the moment your handmade masterpiece finds a home with a satisfied customer, we explore the entire spectrum of craft selling – delving into the art of product creation, establishing a compelling brand presence, and navigating the dynamic landscape of online commerce.

Discover the nuances of setting up your Etsy shop, where each element, from your shop name to your product photography, plays a crucial role in attracting customers. Uncover the secrets of creating compelling product listings that not only captivate potential buyers but also rank high in Etsy's search algorithms.

As we traverse through the chapters, we delve into the intricacies of effective marketing strategies, leveraging social media, and optimizing your shop for search engines to enhance visibility. Learn the art of providing impeccable customer service and building a brand that resonates with your target audience, fostering loyalty and trust.

Navigate the legal and financial considerations that come with running a craft business, from understanding taxes to protecting your intellectual property. Gain insights into scaling your Etsy venture, analyzing shop analytics, and continuous improvement to ensure sustained success.

Whether you are a seasoned artisan or a budding entrepreneur, this guide is crafted to be your companion in the dynamic world of Etsy. Embrace the joy of turning your creative passion into a thriving business, where each crafted piece is not just an item for sale but a story waiting to be told. Welcome to the extraordinary journey of craft selling on Etsy – where creativity knows no bounds, and the possibilities are as endless as your imagination.

Why sell crafts on Etsy:

Selling crafts on Etsy offers a unique and rewarding avenue for artisans and creators. The platform provides a global marketplace where your handmade, vintage, or unique items can find a diverse audience. Etsy's user-friendly interface and established community create an environment conducive to showcasing your craft to enthusiasts worldwide.

Etsy's low barrier to entry allows artisans of all levels to set up shop, providing an accessible platform for emerging talents. The platform's emphasis on handmade and authentic creations resonates with consumers seeking one-of-a-kind items, allowing you to connect with a niche market.

Etsy's robust search and discovery features enhance the visibility of your crafts, increasing the likelihood of attracting potential buyers. The platform's built-in payment and shipping systems simplify transactions, offering a seamless experience for both sellers and customers.

The supportive Etsy community, featuring forums, teams, and events, fosters networking opportunities, collaboration, and continuous learning. Additionally, Etsy's transparent fee structure enables sellers to make informed financial decisions, promoting a fair and sustainable marketplace.

With its global reach, emphasis on authenticity, and commitment to empowering artisans, selling crafts on Etsy not only provides a platform for commerce but also a community-driven space to showcase your creativity and turn your passion into a fulfilling entrepreneurial journey.

Benefits of Esty for crafts sellers

Embarking on the journey of selling crafts on Etsy opens a gateway to a multitude of advantages for artisans and creators alike. Firstly, Etsy serves as a global marketplace, providing unparalleled exposure for your handmade, vintage, or unique creations to a vast and diverse audience.

The user-friendly interface of Etsy simplifies the process of setting up a shop, making it accessible even for newcomers. The platform's low entry barriers democratize entrepreneurship, allowing artisans of varying experience levels to showcase and sell their craft.

Etsy's emphasis on authenticity and handmade items resonates with consumers seeking unique, personalized pieces. This niche focus creates a dedicated community of buyers actively seeking one-of-a-kind items, positioning your crafts in front of an audience with a genuine appreciation for craftsmanship.

The robust search and discovery features on Etsy amplify your crafts' visibility, ensuring that potential buyers can easily find and engage with your products. The integrated payment and shipping systems streamline transactions, providing a hassle-free experience for both sellers and customers.

Moreover, Etsy's commitment to community building extends beyond transactions, fostering a supportive network through forums, teams, and events. This collaborative environment enables artisans to connect, share insights, and learn from each other, contributing to continuous growth and skill enhancement.

The transparency of Etsy's fee structure empowers sellers to make informed financial decisions, promoting fairness and sustainability in the marketplace. Additionally, the platform's commitment to innovation ensures that sellers have access to tools and features that enhance their shops and streamline business operations.

In summary, Etsy stands as more than just a marketplace; it is a thriving ecosystem that celebrates and empowers craftsmen. From global exposure and user-friendly interfaces to a dedicated buyer community and collaborative networking opportunities, Etsy proves to be an invaluable platform for craft sellers, transforming artistic passion into a fulfilling and successful entrepreneurial endeavor.

Understanding Your Target Market On Esty.

Understanding your target market on Etsy is crucial for success in the competitive world of online handmade and vintage goods. Begin by conducting thorough market research to identify your potential customers' demographics, preferences, and buying behaviors.

Utilize Etsy's analytics tools to gain insights into which products are popular and which keywords resonate with your audience.

Consider creating buyer personas to represent your ideal customers, including factors like age, interests, and location. Engage with your target market through social media, forums, and Etsy's own community to build a connection and understand their needs. Monitor reviews and feedback to identify areas for improvement and gauge customer satisfaction.

Tailor your product listings and marketing strategies to align with the interests and values of your target market. Use high-quality images, compelling product descriptions, and relevant tags to enhance visibility. Regularly assess your competitors and stay updated on market trends to remain adaptable.

Building a strong relationship with your target market on Etsy requires ongoing efforts, such as offering promotions, responding promptly to inquiries, and providing exceptional customer service. By continuously refining your understanding of your audience, you can position your Etsy shop for sustained growth and customer loyalty.

Chapter One:

Getting Started On Etsy.

Getting started on Etsy is a straightforward process that begins with creating an account on the platform. Once registered, set up your shop by choosing a catchy and relevant shop name, crafting a compelling bio, and adding a distinctive profile picture. Develop a niche or focus for your shop to stand out in the diverse Etsy marketplace.

Create appealing product listings by using high-quality images, detailed descriptions, and accurate pricing. Leverage Etsy's SEO tools by incorporating relevant keywords in your titles and tags to enhance discoverability. Familiarize yourself with Etsy's policies and guidelines to ensure compliance with the platform's standards.

Establish secure payment methods, set reasonable shipping rates, and consider offering free shipping promotions to attract potential buyers. Engage with the Etsy community by participating in forums, teams, and networking with fellow sellers. Finally, promote your shop through social media and utilize Etsy's advertising options to boost visibility, helping you kickstart your journey on Etsy successfully.

Creating An Esty Account

Creating an Etsy account is a simple process that opens the door to a world of creative entrepreneurship. Begin by visiting the Etsy website and clicking on the "Sign Up" button. Provide a valid email address, or alternatively, use your Google or Facebook account for a seamless registration experience.

Choose a unique username and secure password to protect your account. Once registered, personalize your profile by adding a profile picture and a brief bio to introduce yourself to the Etsy community. Consider sharing your creative journey and inspirations.

Setting Up Your Esty Shop

Setting up your Etsy shop involves several key steps to create a compelling online storefront. Begin by choosing a unique and memorable shop name that reflects your brand. Craft an engaging shop bio, introducing yourself and describing your creative journey. Upload a distinctive profile picture to personalize your brand.

Create product listings with high-quality images that showcase your items from various angles. Write detailed and enticing product descriptions, emphasizing key features and benefits. Set competitive yet profitable prices, considering both production costs and market trends. Utilize relevant tags and keywords in your titles and descriptions to optimize search visibility on Etsy.

Configure secure payment methods for customer transactions, and establish clear shipping policies, including estimated delivery times and rates. Consider offering promotions or free shipping to attract potential buyers. Familiarize yourself with Etsy's policies and guidelines to ensure compliance.

Build trust with customers by promptly responding to inquiries and maintaining excellent customer service. Leverage social media to promote your Etsy shop and connect with a broader audience. Monitor your shop analytics regularly to track performance and make informed business decisions. By following these steps, you can establish a well-crafted Etsy shop that resonates with your target audience and sets the stage for success in the online marketplace.

Crafting An Effective Shop Name

Crafting an effective shop name on Etsy is a crucial step in establishing your brand identity. Choose a name that is not only unique and memorable but also reflective of your products and style. Consider incorporating keywords related to your niche to enhance searchability and attract the right audience.

Ensure your shop name is easy to spell and pronounce, facilitating word-of-mouth promotion. Keep it concise and avoid complex or confusing combinations of words. Conduct a quick search on Etsy to ensure your chosen name is not already in use by another seller.

Inject a touch of creativity and personality into your shop name, making it stand out in the crowded marketplace. Think about the emotions or imagery you want to evoke in potential customers. Remember that your shop name is often the first impression buyers have, so make it inviting and aligned with the essence of your brand.

Lastly, as your business evolves, be open to adjusting your shop name to better align with your brand identity and offerings. A well-crafted shop name not only helps customers remember your brand but also sets the tone for a positive shopping experience on Etsy.

Choosing a profile name and banner for your Etsy shop is a pivotal aspect of creating a compelling and memorable online presence. Your profile name should reflect your brand identity and be easily recognizable. It's advisable to keep it concise, avoiding any complex or confusing combinations. Consider incorporating keywords related to your niche to enhance search visibility and attract your target audience.

Your banner is the visual centerpiece of your Etsy shop, providing an immediate impression of your style and products. Select a banner that aligns with your brand aesthetics, using high-quality images or graphics that represent your offerings. Ensure that the banner complements your profile name and reinforces the overall theme of your shop.

Maintain consistency in design elements across your profile name and banner to create a cohesive and professional look. Utilize colors and fonts that resonate with your brand identity, fostering a visually appealing and memorable storefront. Regularly update your banner to align with seasonal changes, promotions, or new product launches, keeping your shop fresh and engaging for visitors.

Remember that your Etsy profile serves as the face of your business, and a well-thought-out profile name and banner contribute significantly to attracting and retaining customers in the competitive online marketplace.

Choosing a Profile Picture and Banner

Selecting an appealing profile picture and banner is crucial for making a positive first impression on social media platforms. Your profile picture should ideally be a clear, well-lit image of your face, showcasing your personality and professionalism. Ensure that the photo is recent and reflects your current appearance. A genuine smile can go a long way in conveying approachability.

When it comes to choosing a banner or cover photo, consider aligning it with your interests, profession, or personal brand. Use high-resolution images that are visually striking and relevant to the content you share. Maintain a consistent visual theme between your profile picture and banner for a cohesive look. Pay attention to colors and styles that resonate with your personality or brand identity.

Avoid clutter or overly complex visuals that may distract from your main message. Regularly update your profile picture and banner to keep your online presence fresh and reflective of your evolving self. Ultimately, the combination of a captivating profile picture and banner sets the tone for your online persona and can significantly enhance your digital presence.

Understanding Etsy Policies and Guidelines

Understanding Etsy's policies and guidelines is essential for both buyers and sellers to ensure a smooth and secure online marketplace experience. Sellers should familiarize themselves with Etsy's policies regarding product listings, intellectual property, and prohibited items. Adherence to these guidelines helps maintain a trustworthy marketplace.

Buyers, on the other hand, benefit from understanding Etsy's policies on payment, shipping, and returns. Knowing the platform's rules helps buyers make informed decisions, ensures fair transactions, and provides recourse in case of any issues.

Etsy's policies also emphasize the importance of transparent and accurate product representation. Sellers are encouraged to provide detailed item descriptions, clear photographs, and honest information about their products.

Failure to comply with these policies may result in consequences such as account suspension or closure.

To foster a positive community, Etsy encourages open communication between buyers and sellers and provides mechanisms for conflict resolution. Staying informed about these policies not only facilitates successful transactions but also contributes to the overall integrity of the Etsy marketplace.

Copyright and Intellectual Property Guidelines

Understanding and adhering to copyright and intellectual property guidelines is paramount for creators and businesses alike. Copyright protection automatically applies to original works, granting creators exclusive rights to reproduce, distribute, and display their creations. It is crucial to be aware of these rights and respect the intellectual property of others.

When utilizing third-party materials, such as images, music, or written content, ensure proper licensing or permissions are obtained to avoid copyright infringement. Familiarize yourself with fair use and public domain concepts, acknowledging that not all works are subject to the same level of protection.

Registering your creative works with relevant authorities strengthens your legal standing and provides a basis for legal recourse in case of infringement. Clearly mark your creations with copyright notices to communicate your ownership and discourage unauthorized use.

Regularly monitor and enforce your intellectual property rights, taking prompt action against any infringement.

Chapter Two:

Listing Your Crafts

Crafting a compelling online presence for your handmade creations involves strategic and thoughtful listing practices. Begin by selecting a platform that aligns with your target audience and craft niche. Invest time in creating an eye-catching title that succinctly conveys the essence of your product. High-quality product photos are non-negotiable; showcase your crafts from various angles in well-lit environments. Write persuasive and detailed product descriptions, emphasizing the unique qualities, materials used, and the story behind each piece.

Consider optimizing your listing for search engines by incorporating relevant keywords without compromising readability. Highlight any customization options or special features to attract a broader audience. Transparently communicate your pricing structure, ensuring it reflects the value of your craftsmanship. Leverage customer reviews and testimonials to build trust among potential buyers.

Regularly update your inventory to reflect accurate stock levels and introduce fresh creations to keep your store dynamic. Implement a shipping strategy, providing clear information on shipping times and costs. Foster engagement by responding promptly to customer inquiries and encouraging feedback. Utilize social media to cross-promote your listings and connect with a wider audience. Periodically assess and refine your listings based on market trends, customer feedback, and evolving creative directions. This dynamic approach ensures that your craft listings remain appealing and relevant in the competitive online marketplace.

High-Quality Product Photos

Capturing the essence of your products through high-quality photos is a cornerstone of successful online sales. Invest time and resources in professional photography or learn basic techniques to ensure clear, well-composed images. Adequate lighting is crucial; natural light or diffused artificial light can enhance details and colors, showcasing your products in the best possible way.

Utilize various angles to provide a comprehensive view, allowing potential customers to appreciate the craftsmanship. Choose backgrounds that complement your products without distracting from them, maintaining a cohesive visual theme across your listings. Pay attention to composition and framing, ensuring the focus remains on the product itself.

Consistency in photo style across your product range creates a polished and professional look for your online store. Optimize image resolution to accommodate zoom features, allowing customers to scrutinize details. Showcase any unique features, textures, or intricate elements to highlight the craftsmanship.

High-quality product photos not only attract attention but also instill confidence in potential buyers, offering a virtual experience that closely mirrors an in-person examination. Regularly update your images to keep your listings fresh, reflecting any changes or improvements to your products. Ultimately, the visual appeal of your product photos significantly influences the perception and desirability of your handmade crafts.

Writing Persuasive Product Descriptions

The words you choose can make or break a sale. Craft compelling product descriptions that go beyond stating features, conveying the unique story and benefits of your crafts. Use descriptive language, evoke emotions, and highlight the value your handmade items bring to customers. Include details about materials, dimensions, and care instructions, ensuring potential buyers have all the information they need to make an informed purchase.

Setting the Right Prices

Determining the right pricing strategy is crucial for the success of your craft business. Conduct market research to understand competitors' pricing, factor in production costs, and consider the perceived value of your handmade products. Finding a balance between competitiveness and profitability is key. Clearly communicate the value proposition to customers, justifying the price based on the craftsmanship, uniqueness, and quality of your creations.

Managing Inventory and Stocking Options

Efficient inventory management is essential for a successful craft business. Regularly update your online listings to reflect accurate stock levels. Consider creating a sense of urgency by showcasing limited editions or seasonal items. Explore options for made-to-order or customizable crafts to offer variety without overstocking. Implementing a reliable inventory tracking system ensures you can meet customer demand while avoiding unnecessary overproduction. Regularly reassess and adjust your stocking options based on sales trends and customer preferences

Creating Compelling Product Listings

Crafting an effective product listing is an art that goes beyond a mere showcase; it's a persuasive tool to engage and convert potential customers. Begin with a captivating title that succinctly communicates the essence of your product. High-quality, visually appealing images are critical—showcase your product from various angles, utilizing proper lighting to highlight details. Provide a detailed and compelling product description that not only lists features but also narrates the unique story and benefits of your creation.

Employ persuasive language that evokes emotions and creates a connection with the buyer. Clearly communicate essential details such as materials used, dimensions, and care instructions. Consider incorporating relevant keywords for search engine optimization to enhance visibility. Transparently present pricing, justifying it with the craftsmanship and value your product offers. Utilize customer reviews and testimonials to build trust and credibility.

Create a sense of urgency or exclusivity by highlighting limited editions or seasonal relevance. Implement cross-selling strategies by suggesting related products, encouraging customers to explore your full range. Regularly update your listings to reflect new additions or modifications based on customer feedback and market trends. Consistency in branding and presentation across all listings contributes to a cohesive and memorable online store experience, enhancing your chances of attracting and retaining customers.

Chapter Three:

Optimizing your Esty Shop

Optimizing your Etsy shop involves strategic steps to enhance visibility and attract buyers. Begin by selecting relevant and popular tags for your listings, incorporating trending keywords. Craft compelling product titles that resonate with your target audience, and invest in professional, well-lit product photography to showcase your items. Write detailed, SEO-friendly descriptions that answer potential buyer questions, and ensure competitive pricing by researching your market. Organize your shop into clear sections for easy navigation and engage with customers through prompt communication to build positive relationships. Regularly update your shop with new listings and promotions, leveraging Etsy's analytics tools to gain insights into customer behavior. Encourage customer reviews to build trust, and consider cross-promotion strategies to boost sales. Share your listings on social media platforms, integrating them into a broader online presence. Clearly communicate shipping policies and explore Etsy's advertising options to maximize product visibility. Lastly, maintain transparency with well-defined shop policies, fostering trust with customers and contributing to the overall success of your Etsy venture.

Enhancing Your Shop's SEO:

To enhance your shop's SEO, focus on creating a cohesive and organized storefront. Utilize relevant keywords throughout your product listings, titles, and descriptions. Consider conducting regular keyword research to stay abreast of evolving search trends in your niche. Beyond keywords, ensure that your shop maintains a consistent branding strategy, as Etsy's algorithm considers this when ranking search results. Optimize your product images for search by using clear, high-quality photos and adding alt text. Regularly update your inventory, and encourage customer reviews, as both factors contribute positively to your shop's search ranking.

Choosing the Right Keywords:

Selecting the right keywords is a fundamental step in SEO success. Conduct thorough research using tools like Google Keyword Planner to identify high-performing keywords relevant to your products. Diversify your keyword selection by including both short and long-tail variations. Pay attention to seasonal or trending terms within your niche, and incorporate these keywords naturally into your product titles, descriptions, and tags for maximum impact on your shop's discoverability.

Updating Titles and Descriptions for SEO:

Regularly updating product titles and descriptions is essential for maintaining a strong SEO presence. Ensure your titles are clear, concise, and contain relevant keywords. Craft detailed and informative product descriptions that not only appeal to customers but also contribute to search engine optimization. Use language that addresses potential buyer queries and concerns. Strive for readability while incorporating strategic keywords seamlessly, keeping in mind the evolving nature of search algorithms.

Utilizing Etsy's Marketing Tools:

Etsy provides an array of marketing tools to boost your shop's visibility. Experiment with features such as sales and discounts, offering enticing promotions to attract customers. Implement coupon codes strategically to incentivize repeat business. Leverage these tools based on your specific product offerings and target audience, while keeping an eye on analytics to refine your marketing strategy over time.

Promoted Listings:

Take advantage of Promoted Listings to elevate your products within Etsy's search results. Set a competitive daily budget and bid strategically for ad placement. Regularly analyze the performance metrics provided by Etsy to fine-tune your advertising strategy. Consider targeting specific high-performing products or seasonal items to maximize the impact of your promoted listings.

Etsy Ads:

Etsy Ads provide an opportunity to extend your reach beyond the platform. Create targeted advertising campaigns with defined budgets and audience parameters. Monitor the performance of your ads regularly and adjust your strategy based on the provided analytics. Consider experimenting with different ad formats to identify the most effective approach for your unique products and customer base.

Implementing Social Media Strategies for Promotion

Implementing these comprehensive strategies collectively will not only enhance your Etsy shop's visibility but also contribute to sustained growth and increased sales. Regularly assess performance metrics and adapt your approach to align with market dynamics and evolving customer behaviors.

In today's dynamic digital landscape, implementing effective social media strategies is paramount for successful promotion. Begin by defining clear objectives, whether it's brand awareness, engagement, or lead generation. Understand your target audience and choose platforms where they are most active.

Craft compelling content that resonates with your audience, blending creativity with consistency. Leverage multimedia elements such as videos, images, and infographics to enhance engagement. Utilize relevant hashtags to expand reach and join conversations within your industry.

Establish a consistent posting schedule, considering optimal times for your audience. Encourage user-generated content to foster a sense of community. Monitor analytics to track performance, adjusting strategies based on real-time insights.

Engage with your audience through comments, messages, and polls, fostering a two-way communication channel. Collaborate with influencers to amplify your reach and credibility. Implement paid advertising strategically to target specific demographics.

Stay abreast of social media trends and algorithm changes, adapting your strategies accordingly. Foster a positive online reputation by addressing customer feedback promptly. Continuously refine your approach based on data, ensuring your social media promotion remains agile and effective in a rapidly evolving digital landscape.

Chapter Four:

Providing Excellent Customer Service.

Providing excellent customer service is the cornerstone of a successful business. It begins with active listening to understand customers' needs and concerns. Respond promptly and courteously, demonstrating empathy and a genuine desire to assist.

Consistency is key—strive to deliver a consistent level of service across all interactions and touchpoints. Anticipate customer needs and go the extra mile to exceed expectations, fostering loyalty and positive word-of-mouth.

Empower your frontline staff with the knowledge and tools to resolve issues efficiently. Implement a user-friendly customer support system, including accessible channels like live chat, email, and phone support.

Personalization adds a personalized touch to interactions—use customer data to tailor experiences and recommendations. Seek feedback actively and use it to enhance your services continuously.

Address problems transparently, admitting mistakes if they occur, and provide swift resolutions. Train your team to handle challenging situations with grace, turning potential negatives into positive experiences.

Ultimately, exceptional customer service builds trust, strengthens brand reputation, and cultivates long-lasting relationships with customers.

Responding to Customer Inquiries:

Mastering the art of responding to customer inquiries requires a comprehensive strategy that prioritizes swift, personalized, and empathetic communication. Implementing a multichannel approach, including email, live chat, and social media, ensures accessibility for a diverse customer base. Leverage technology for automated responses to routine queries, freeing up human resources for more complex interactions. Regularly review and update FAQs to empower customers with self-service options. Emphasize a solution-oriented approach, aiming not just to resolve inquiries but to exceed customer expectations and leave a lasting positive impression.

Handling Orders and Shipping:

The efficient management of orders and shipping is pivotal to the overall customer experience. Provide real-time tracking information, estimated delivery times, and clear communication regarding any delays. Optimize order processing workflows to ensure accuracy, timeliness, and a seamless customer journey. Offer flexible shipping options, transparent cost breakdowns, and consider implementing loyalty programs that include perks like discounted or expedited shipping. Proactively address issues such as out-of-stock items or backorders, demonstrating transparency and commitment to customer satisfaction throughout the entire order fulfillment process.

Managing Customer Reviews and Feedback:

A robust approach to managing customer reviews and feedback involves actively participating in online conversations, showcasing responsiveness and dedication to continuous improvement. Encourage customers to share their experiences across various platforms, both positive and negative. Respond promptly to reviews, expressing gratitude for positive feedback and presenting concrete solutions for any negative comments. Integrate customer insights into your product or service development process, emphasizing an adaptive and customer-centric business model. Utilize feedback to refine marketing strategies, ensuring that your brand perception aligns with customer expectations. Regularly monitor and analyze customer sentiment to proactively address emerging trends or concerns, reinforcing your commitment to an evolving and customer-driven business approach.

Chapter Five:

Legal and Financial Considerations.

Navigating the legal and financial landscape is integral to the success and sustainability of any business. Establishing a solid legal foundation involves choosing the right business structure, adhering to industry regulations, and securing necessary licenses. Compliance with local, state, and federal laws is paramount, covering areas such as employment, intellectual property, and data protection.

Financial considerations encompass prudent budgeting, accurate accounting practices, and strategic financial planning. Maintaining transparent financial records is crucial for tax compliance and investor confidence. Businesses should regularly assess their cash flow, manage debt responsibly, and explore avenues for sustainable growth. Risk management strategies, including insurance coverage, help mitigate unforeseen challenges.

Employee contracts and vendor agreements should be meticulously drafted, outlining terms and responsibilities. Businesses should also safeguard their intellectual property through patents, trademarks, and copyrights. Regular legal audits and consultations with financial experts can ensure ongoing compliance and fortify the organization against potential legal or financial pitfalls, fostering long-term stability and success.

Understanding Taxes for Etsy Sellers:

For Etsy sellers, comprehending tax obligations is essential for a successful and legally compliant business. Different jurisdictions may have varying tax requirements, including sales tax, income tax, and possibly even international tax implications. Sellers must keep meticulous records of income and expenses, separating personal and business finances. Familiarizing oneself with tax deductions applicable to creative enterprises, such as materials and shipping costs, is crucial for optimizing financial outcomes. Regularly updating knowledge on tax regulations and seeking professional advice can ensure accurate filings and prevent legal complications. Etsy provides resources and tools to help sellers navigate tax responsibilities, and staying informed about changes in tax laws is paramount to maintaining a thriving and financially sound Etsy shop.

Complying with Local and International Regulations:

Etsy sellers operating in a global marketplace must navigate a complex landscape of local and international regulations to ensure legal compliance. Understanding and adhering to local business licensing requirements, sales tax regulations, and import/export rules is crucial. Complying with international trade regulations, such as customs and duties, is imperative for seamless cross-border transactions. Sellers must stay informed about changes in regulations and seek legal advice when expanding into new markets. Cultivating awareness of consumer protection laws and privacy regulations is essential for building trust with customers worldwide. Regular audits and assessments of compliance with local and international regulations are fundamental practices for sustaining a reputable and legally secure Etsy business.

Protecting Your Intellectual Property:

Preserving intellectual property is paramount for Etsy sellers, given the creative nature of their products. Registering trademarks, copyrights, or patents provides legal protection against unauthorized use or reproduction of original designs. Regularly monitoring the marketplace for potential infringements and promptly addressing any violations is crucial to safeguarding intellectual property. Crafting clear and comprehensive contracts with collaborators, suppliers, and manufacturers can establish ownership and usage rights. Utilizing Etsy's Intellectual Property Policy and reporting mechanisms can aid in resolving disputes and protecting creative assets. Staying informed about the legal landscape related to intellectual property, including changes in copyright or trademark laws, is essential for proactive protection. Developing a proactive strategy for intellectual property protection not only safeguards the seller's creations but also fosters a secure and reputable brand on the Etsy platform.

Chapter Six:

Continuous Improvement and Growth

Continuous improvement and growth are integral components of a thriving and adaptable business model. Embracing a culture of continuous improvement involves regularly evaluating processes, identifying inefficiencies, and implementing strategic changes. This iterative approach fosters innovation, enhances operational efficiency, and ensures that the organization remains agile in a dynamic market.

Feedback from customers, employees, and stakeholders plays a pivotal role in driving continuous improvement initiatives. By actively seeking and responding to input, businesses can address concerns, capitalize on strengths, and refine products or services to meet evolving demands.

Investing in employee training and development is key to sustaining growth. A skilled and motivated workforce contributes to increased productivity and innovative problem-solving. Encouraging a mindset of learning and adaptation throughout the organization nurtures resilience in the face of challenges.

Regularly assessing market trends, competition, and emerging technologies allows businesses to stay ahead of the curve. This proactive approach enables strategic decision-making, helping organizations pivot and capitalize on new opportunities for expansion and diversification.

In essence, the pursuit of continuous improvement and growth is not merely a goal but a dynamic process that requires commitment, flexibility, and a forward-thinking mindset to ensure sustained success in an ever-evolving business landscape

Analyzing Shop Analytics:

Delving into shop analytics is a crucial practice for Etsy sellers aiming to understand and enhance their online businesses. Etsy provides a wealth of data, including views, clicks, and conversion rates, offering insights into customer behavior. Sellers should scrutinize these analytics to identify popular products, optimal posting times, and the effectiveness of marketing efforts. By leveraging this information, sellers can refine their product offerings, pricing strategies, and promotional activities. Analyzing the performance of keywords and tags can also boost visibility in search results, ultimately driving more traffic and sales. Regularly monitoring shop analytics empowers Etsy sellers to make data-driven decisions, adapt to market trends, and optimize their online presence for sustained success.

Gathering Customer Feedback for Improvement:

Customer feedback is a goldmine of insights for Etsy sellers striving to enhance their products and services. Actively soliciting and analyzing feedback provides valuable information about customer preferences, satisfaction levels, and areas for improvement. Utilizing platforms like Etsy reviews and surveys helps sellers gauge the market perception of their products and identifies opportunities for refinement. Positive feedback can be highlighted in marketing efforts, while constructive criticism should be viewed as a roadmap for product enhancements. Promptly addressing customer concerns and implementing suggested improvements not only boosts customer satisfaction but also contributes to the long-term success and reputation of an Etsy business. Consistent communication and a customer-centric approach based on gathered feedback foster trust and loyalty, turning buyers into repeat customers.

Scaling Your Etsy Business

:Scaling your Etsy business is a strategic endeavor that involves careful planning, innovation, and a commitment to long-term success. Begin by assessing the scalability of your products and processes. Ensure that your production capacity, supply chain, and fulfillment capabilities can handle an increase in demand without compromising quality. Diversify your product offerings to appeal to a broader audience, considering trends and customer preferences.

Expanding your market reach is crucial for scaling. Explore new markets and demographics, both locally and internationally, to tap into a larger customer base. Implement targeted marketing campaigns, leveraging social media, email marketing, and collaborations to enhance brand visibility. Optimize your pricing strategy to accommodate growth, balancing competitiveness with profitability.

Efficient inventory management is essential when scaling. Implement systems to track and manage stock levels, preventing stockouts or excess inventory. Consider partnerships with suppliers to ensure a stable and reliable source of materials. Automation can streamline processes, reducing manual workload and minimizing errors as your business expands.

Customer satisfaction remains paramount during scaling. Maintain a strong focus on delivering quality products and exceptional customer service. Utilize customer feedback to refine your offerings and address any issues promptly. A positive reputation is crucial for sustaining growth and attracting repeat business.

Financial management becomes increasingly complex when scaling. Regularly analyze financial metrics, track expenses, and monitor cash flow to ensure financial stability. Explore financing options if necessary, and seek professional advice to navigate the complexities of business expansion.

Continuous monitoring and adaptation are key. Regularly review performance metrics, market trends, and customer feedback. Stay agile and be ready to adjust strategies based on evolving circumstances. This dynamic approach ensures that your Etsy business not only scales successfully but also maintains a competitive edge in the ever-changing e-commerce landscape.

Chapter Seven:

Troubleshooting Common Issues.

Troubleshooting common issues is a critical skill for maintaining smooth business operations. Begin by identifying the root cause of the problem through thorough investigation and analysis. Often, effective troubleshooting involves understanding the context, asking pertinent questions, and utilizing diagnostic tools.

Communication is key during the troubleshooting process. Keep stakeholders informed about the issue, its potential impact, and the steps being taken to resolve it. Establish clear and transparent channels for reporting problems and encourage a culture of open communication within the team.

Prioritize issues based on their impact on business functions, addressing high-priority concerns first. Implement a systematic approach, breaking down complex problems into manageable steps. Document the troubleshooting process for future reference, creating a knowledge base that aids in resolving similar issues efficiently.

Collaborate with team members, drawing on diverse expertise to solve multifaceted problems. Emphasize preventive measures to mitigate the recurrence of common issues, such as implementing software updates, conducting regular maintenance, and providing ongoing training.

Regularly review and update troubleshooting procedures as technologies and business processes evolve. By cultivating a proactive troubleshooting mindset and fostering a collaborative environment, businesses can navigate challenges effectively and ensure uninterrupted productivity.

Dealing with Order Issues:

Effectively handling order issues is paramount for maintaining customer satisfaction and the reputation of your business. When customers encounter problems such as delayed shipments or damaged products, respond promptly and empathetically. Establish a clear and accessible customer support system to address concerns through various channels, including email and live chat.

Implement a transparent and fair return and refund policy, communicating these terms clearly on your platform. Provide step-by-step guidance for customers on how to resolve common order issues, ensuring a smooth and hassle-free experience. Collaborate with your shipping partners to minimize delivery hiccups and keep customers informed about the status of their orders.

Use order data and analytics to identify patterns and proactively address recurring issues. By staying attentive to customer feedback, you can continuously improve your processes and prevent similar problems in the future. A proactive and customer-centric approach to order issues not only resolves immediate concerns but also builds trust and loyalty.

Addressing Negative Reviews:

Negative reviews can be challenging, but addressing them professionally and constructively is key to maintaining a positive brand image. Respond promptly to negative reviews, expressing gratitude for the feedback and demonstrating a commitment to resolving the issue. Avoid being defensive; instead, focus on finding solutions and ensuring customer satisfaction.

Encourage customers to contact you directly to discuss their concerns privately. This shows other potential customers that you are proactive in resolving issues. When appropriate, offer a thoughtful and genuine apology, along with concrete steps you are taking to prevent similar problems in the future.

Use negative reviews as an opportunity to showcase your dedication to customer service. By addressing issues publicly and transparently, you demonstrate authenticity and accountability. Consider implementing a review management strategy that emphasizes positive interactions with customers and encourages them to share their positive experiences.

Handling Copyright and Trademark Concerns:

Navigating copyright and trademark concerns is crucial to protecting your intellectual property and maintaining legal compliance. Conduct thorough research before using any design or content to ensure it does not infringe on existing copyrights or trademarks. If in doubt, seek legal advice to avoid potential legal ramifications.

Secure copyrights and trademarks for your original creations to safeguard your intellectual property. Monitor the market for any unauthorized use of your brand or products and take prompt legal action when necessary. Regularly audit your own practices to ensure compliance with intellectual property laws.

Educate your team on copyright and trademark regulations, fostering a culture of respect for intellectual property. If you receive a notice of infringement, address it promptly and professionally. Implement stringent procedures for vetting new designs and content to prevent unintentional violations.

By proactively managing copyright and trademark concerns, businesses can protect their brand integrity, avoid legal disputes, and foster an environment that respects intellectual property rights.

Chapter Eight:

Case Study on an Etsy Craft Seller's Journey

In this comprehensive case study, we delve into the inspiring journey of Jane Doe, a successful Etsy craft seller, to uncover the strategies and practices that propelled her shop to remarkable success. Jane's story serves as an insightful blueprint for aspiring entrepreneurs seeking to establish and thrive in the competitive world of online crafting.

Background:

Jane Doe began her Etsy venture in 2016, driven by her passion for handcrafted home decor. With a background in graphic design, she carefully curated a collection of personalized items that stood out in the crowded Etsy marketplace. Her commitment to quality, uniqueness, and customer satisfaction set the foundation for her shop's success.

Product Differentiation:

A key factor in Jane's success was her ability to differentiate her products. Through meticulous research and a keen understanding of market trends, she identified gaps in the market and developed products that filled those niches. Personalized and customizable items quickly became her shop's hallmark, attracting a niche customer base seeking unique, one-of-a-kind pieces.

Branding and Photography:

Jane invested time and effort into crafting a compelling brand identity that resonated with her target audience. Consistent branding across her Etsy shop, social media platforms, and packaging enhanced the overall customer experience. High-quality, professionally photographed product images showcased her creations in the best light, contributing to increased visibility and sales.

Effective Marketing Strategies:

Jane embraced a multi-faceted marketing approach, utilizing Etsy's platform features and external channels. Strategic use of keywords, leveraging Etsy ads, and participating in seasonal promotions boosted her shop's visibility within the marketplace. Active engagement on social media platforms and collaborations with influencers expanded her reach beyond Etsy, attracting a broader customer base.

Customer Engagement and Satisfaction:

Jane prioritized customer engagement and satisfaction, fostering a loyal customer community. Personalized thank-you notes, timely responses to inquiries, and a seamless order fulfillment process contributed to positive reviews and repeat business. By actively listening to customer feedback, she implemented improvements, solidifying her shop's reputation for exceptional service.

Adaptability and Continuous Learning:

Jane remained adaptable to changing market dynamics and consumer preferences. Regularly analyzing shop analytics, staying informed about Etsy updates, and attending industry events kept her abreast of evolving trends. This adaptability allowed her to introduce new products, refine strategies, and stay ahead of the competition.

Community Engagement:

Active participation in the Etsy community played a pivotal role in Jane's success. Engaging in forums, joining seller groups, and participating in virtual events fostered a sense of camaraderie. Collaborations with fellow sellers and mentorship opportunities provided additional support and insights.

Jane Doe's journey as a successful Etsy craft seller offers a comprehensive view of the strategies and practices that contributed to her remarkable achievements. From product differentiation and effective marketing to customer engagement and community involvement, her story serves as an invaluable resource for Etsy sellers aspiring to carve their own path to success in the dynamic world of online crafting.

Frequently Asked Questions (FAQ)

❖ What types of crafts can I sell on Etsy?

Etsy accommodates a wide range of crafts, including handmade jewelry, clothing, art, home decor, vintage items, and digital downloads. Ensure your products comply with Etsy's policies.

❖ How do I set up a shop on Etsy?

Creating an Etsy shop involves signing up for an account, choosing a shop name, and listing your items. Follow Etsy's step-by-step guide to set up your shop profile, policies, and payment methods.

❖ . What are the fees associated with selling on Etsy?

Etsy charges a listing fee for each product, a transaction fee on each sale, and, if applicable, a payment processing fee. Familiarize yourself with Etsy's fee structure to understand the costs associated with selling.

❖ How can I optimize my product listings for better visibility?

Use high-quality photos, craft compelling product descriptions with relevant keywords, and set competitive pricing. Regularly update listings, and utilize tags effectively to improve search visibility.

❖ How does shipping work on Etsy?

You can choose to ship globally or limit your shipping locations. Set accurate shipping costs, processing times, and provide tracking information to keep customers informed.

❖ What is the importance of customer reviews on Etsy?

Customer reviews are crucial for building trust. Positive reviews enhance your shop's reputation, attracting more customers. Address negative reviews professionally and work towards resolutions.

❖ How do I handle custom orders?

Clearly communicate your ability to handle custom orders in your shop policies. Discuss details with customers, set realistic expectations, and create custom listings for payment.

❖ Can I sell vintage items on Etsy?

Yes, Etsy allows the sale of vintage items that are at least 20 years old. Ensure accurate product descriptions, clear photographs, and adherence to Etsy's guidelines for vintage selling.

❖ How do I market my Etsy shop outside the platform?

Utilize social media platforms, create a blog, and participate in local craft fairs to promote your Etsy shop. Engage with your target audience and utilize digital marketing strategies for broader reach.

❖ How can I handle sales tax for my Etsy shop?

Understand the sales tax regulations in your location and Etsy's rules regarding tax collection. Etsy can automatically calculate and collect sales tax for certain transactions based on the buyer's location.

❖ How can I stay updated on Etsy policies and changes?

Regularly check Etsy's Seller Handbook and stay informed about policy updates through email notifications and Etsy's community forums. Participate in webinars and virtual events hosted by Etsy for additional insights.

❖ . Are there any restrictions on intellectual property and copyright?

Yes, Etsy has strict policies on intellectual property. Ensure that your products do not infringe on copyrights, trademarks, or patents. Research and follow Etsy's guidelines to avoid legal issues.

❖ How do I handle disputes with customers?

Respond promptly to customer inquiries and address issues professionally. If disputes arise, work towards resolutions and, if necessary, involve Etsy's customer support for assistance.

❖ Can I collaborate with other Etsy sellers?

Yes, collaboration is encouraged. Engage with other sellers through Etsy teams, participate in joint promotions, and consider cross-promoting each other's products to expand your reach.

❖ How can I improve my Etsy shop's SEO?

Research relevant keywords for your products, include them in your product titles and tags, and regularly update your listings. Utilize Etsy's SEO features to enhance your shop's visibility in search results.